Off to the
CIRCUS

Om
KIDZ
An imprint of Om Books International

Reprinted in 2018

Corporate & Editorial Office
A-12, Sector 64, Noida 201 301
Uttar Pradesh, India
Phone: +91 120 477 4100
Email: editorial@ombooks.com
Website: www.ombooksinternational.com

Sales Office
107, Ansari Road, Darya Ganj
New Delhi 110 002, India
Phone: +91 11 4000 9000
Email: sales@ombooks.com
Website: www.ombooks.com

ISBN: 978-93-86108-87-6

Printed in India

10 9 8 7 6 5 4 3 2

Off to the CIRCUS

I'm all set to read

Paste your photograph here

My name is

478, HAMILTON ROAD
EVERY DAY AT 4 PM

Amy was walking in **the** park.

She liked **the** fresh **air**.

All of a sudden, **she saw** a paper.

SUN
CIRCUS
478, HAMILTON
EVERY DAY AT

The paper **was** an ad **for the** circus. It **was** full of colours. "**SUN** CIRCUS" **was** written on **top**. There were clowns **and** colourful tents on it.

Amy took **the** paper to **her** mother.

"**Mom**, **can** we please go to **the** circus?" **she** asked **her** mother.

Amy’s **mom** read **the** ad.

“We **can** go this Sunday. **But you** must finish your homework every **day** this week,” **she** said.

"Yay!" Amy let out a **cry** of **joy**.

She worked hard **all** week.

Finally, on Sunday, **Mom** took **her** to circus in **the car**.

The circus **was** inside a **big**, colourful tent.

It **had** many chairs **for** people to **sit**.

Amy and her mom sat on **two** of **the** chairs.

The circus began with a **lot** of music.

A **man** wearing a **hat** stood in **the** middle of **the** stage.

“Welcome to **the** circus!” he called **out**. “Meet **our** friends **Pep**, **Pop and Pip**.”

Pep, **Pop and Pip** were **the** circus clowns.

They wore colourful clothes **and had** round, **red** noses.

They wore **big**, **red** shoes.

The clowns began to juggle colourful balls.

They threw **the** balls at each other.

They even bounced **the** balls **off** their heads!

All of a sudden, **Pip** threw a **pie** at **Pep**'s face.

All the people burst **out** laughing.

Amy was having a **lot** of **fun**.

The trapeze artists were next.

They swung from **one rod** to another, high in **the air**.

They jumped **and** twirled **mid-air**.

"**Aah**!" said **the** crowd in **awe**.

The acrobats performed after that. They were so good!

Finally, **the** circus came to an **end**.

Amy and Mom left **the** circus tent feeling very happy.

It **was** a **fun** Sunday at **the** circus.

Which clown does the hat belong to? Circle that clown.

Colour the balls with three-letter words.

Match the circus people to their shadows.

Know your words

Sight Words

was	two	joy	end
the	lot	for	yay
air	can	big	mid
had	but	red	
all	you	off	
she	day	fun	
and	let	one	
her	out	awe	

Naming Words

Amy	Mom	Pop	hat
sun	Pip	pie	car
top	Pep	rod	man

Doing Words

saw	cry	sit	sat